BRISTOL BLACK& WHITE

MARK SIMMONS

Published 2008 by Tangent Books

Unit 5.16 Paintworks

Arnos Vale

Bristol

BS4 3EH

0117 972 0645

www.tangentbooks.co.uk

richard@tangentbooks.co.uk

Bristol Black & White

ISBN 9781906477141

Design: **Joe Burt**

Packaged by: **Faragher Jones**

www.faragherjones.com

Publisher: **Richard Jones**

Thanks to: **Steve Wright**

For my mum Joan Simmons (April 1929-April 2007) whose kind heart and social conscience inspired me. Also, for my lovely dad Fred (Tim to his mates), Melina and Jacob and to all my friends and family who are more special than they know. Thanks to Martin Barnard (Warm Tone), David Hall (Blue Sky Images), Steve and Scott at Headroom, Steve Wright and all at Tangent for the production of this book.

FOREWORD *04-05*
INTRODUCTION *06-09*

FOREWORD *by Mark Simmons*

These images are a collection of some of my favourite social documentary photographs and portraits taken over the last 25 years.

Looking back, it was quite lucky how I got into photography. My inspiration was my Uncle Bill who gave me my first 35mm camera. Then, when I moved to Bristol, a university friend called Adam taught me how to develop and print film in the darkroom.

After completing my degree in chemistry, I applied myself in earnest to the job of recording life around me. I found it empowering and never lost the excitement of being able to press the shutter of my Nikon and capture a slice of life for posterity.

Going into the darkroom later to develop the film was almost as exciting – seeing what I'd captured as I looked through the rolls of freshly developed negatives. I can't imagine how much of my life I've spent in the dark!

In those early days I used to carry my camera with me wherever I went. This resulted in many of the 'Street' photographs that appear in the first chapter of this book. For me, there has always been a fascination in photographing ordinary people and bringing out that spark, mystery – something special that we all have but rarely show the outside world. My desire to combine this approach to recording life – along with strong compositions and interesting narratives – has driven my image making.

As well as working in the general areas of community, arts, education, performance and music, I undertook two long-term documentary projects. The first was following protests and demonstrations, particularly the anti-Poll Tax movement of 1990/91. The second was a major five-year study of different faith groups in Bristol with fellow photographer and artist Jan Pemberton. This led to a main gallery exhibition at Watershed media centre in 1992/93, a touring exhibition and an educational programme. Both of these works are represented in this book.

Photography plays a major role in shaping the way we see the world. We are constantly bombarded by imagery across all media. This usually conforms to a few main genres such as fashion and advertising, voyeuristic paparazzi shots, cheesy press snaps in local papers, and 'soft' and 'hard' news photographs reinforcing the general climate of apprehension but never showing the full horror of subjects such as war.

There is little that is real in any of these portrayals, but there are other types of photographs that don't have such a high profile through the mass media, but which capture real life with poignancy and passion. It is this area of reportage photography that has most influenced and inspired me. In particular, the tradition of street photography which aims to capture the ordinary and the extraordinary in life around us, in a way that brings power to these moments and a dignity to those captured. Photographs are really only illustrative of life because they are (to varying degrees) a construct of the photographer; yet they are often read as real interpretations of events or how things are.

There is a convention that you are not supposed to have smiling faces or people looking directly at the camera in serious documentary images - but why not? Is this not as real as the images of people looking away, distant, awkward, bored or weird?

The science of quantum mechanics reveals that the observer and the observed are intrinsically connected. Therefore, rather than being dispassionate witnesses of a world in which we play no part, perhaps there is a way of seeing and engaging in our world – based on compassion for our fellow beings – that could truly connect all of us.

Let's not deceive ourselves (however tempting and romantic the notion) that we can glance unobserved into the lives of others.

Mark Simmons
Bristol 2008

INTRODUCTION *by Steve Wright*

"At the start, people are usually curious – they wonder why on earth you want to photograph them. But they're also flattered, especially if they sense that your motives are honest. That's the beginning of the relationship. I just want people to relax and show me something of themselves."

You can always see how much at ease Mark Simmons' subjects are from the bold, unflinching gaze they send back at the viewer – welcoming and colluding with us, inviting us into the world of the picture.

Humans are generally self-conscious – especially when it comes to having their photograph taken – but they don't look that way in Mark's photographs. How so?

"There's nothing very complicated to it: I just generally like people," Mark continues. "That's not to say that it's easy getting a good picture of someone: it's

very difficult. But it's about finding a way to connect with people. And that's about being sensitive to their particular character and story."

There's also something unerringly positive and respectful about these images: Mark looks for and finds the best in people, and invariably captures his subjects at their most creative, expressive and unguarded. "I just try to put people at ease, get a relationship going," he explains. "I want positive images, but also images that tell you something meaningful – not just about these people, but about the human condition in general."

Leafing through this collection, you'll see personalities everywhere, uninhibited and unshackled. I have seen very few pouting, unhappy faces in Mark's portraits, and though that may sound trite it means something – both that he is looking for the positive

wherever he can find it, and also that he is able to put his subjects at ease.

There's a message in there, too, about the dignity of everyday life – how all our real, day-to-day passions (music, dance, festivals, religion) and bugbears (from prejudice to the Poll Tax) are somehow more interesting – more real, more beautiful – than the airbrushed beauties and longed-for lives that fill our magazines and advertising hoardings. "The positive imagery we get from advertising is superficial, fake," Mark reflects. "I like to find ordinary people looking good, interesting, powerful."

He believes strongly in the values of ordinary people, in the power of large, spontaneous public gatherings and in the emotive force of community events.

Mark has a talent for injecting drama into the everyday. He crouches low on the pavement to shoot an old man and his dog, giving them an elevated, almost heroic prospect, an epic sweep, a sense of grandeur among the very everyday urban surroundings of Bristol's Lawrence Hill. He is fascinated by whatever his subjects are fascinated by: that state of religious fervour, almost grace, that any of us can attain when completely absorbed in whatever we are doing (it's no coincidence that Mark spent some five years documenting Bristol's various religious communities).

The youth's face takes on an angelic glow as he stares, rapt, into the bowels of the fruit machine; high on a parapet of scaffolding, the Poll Tax protester urges the masses forward with Messianic fervour; the teenager getting an initiation into the pleasures of dance looks totally absorbed, lost in his own world. These are people utterly involved in what normal life has offered them or thrown in their path.

To say that 'every picture tells a story' is a cliché: in these pictures, though, there's a definite narrative arc, a sense of movement and direction. Look at the way the huge mechanical claw stoops towards the scrapyard worker – as if pausing millimetres from his back to accentuate the drama, the sense of a moment poised.

This book's last chapter 'People' showcases this storytelling ethos in subtly different ways. Among the subjects pictured here are a clutch of characters – Massive Attack, Rob Smith of Smith & Mighty, Roni Size and Krust who had a huge impact on the nascent Bristol Sound – aka trip hop, which was to become one of the defining musical currents of the 1990s. Here, too, there is drama and narrative, but not in the obvious ways we might expect: these are new sides to perhaps familiar faces.

At the gates of his old school Massive's 3D turns away from the camera, head bowed like a fifth-form rebel, a global megastar reduced to (and somehow humanised by) these homelier circumstances. Rob Smith's face is half-obscured by darkness, somehow appropriate for someone who played such a crucial role in the Bristol Sound's development yet who remains, relative to the likes of Massive, Portishead, little known to a wider audience.

Most of Mark's subjects, though, are working-class people out on the street living normal, unglamorous lives. "I'm fascinated by body language, how expressive it can be and how you can use it to read people," he explains. "Normal, ordinary, working-class folk are very open with their body language. Middle-class people tend to be more guarded, more self-conscious."

Tellingly, a lot of the shots are taken in the street, in community centres, at neighbourhood or city-wide events. These are lives that people are making for themselves, not events foisted on them by big corporations. There are no shots here of rooms full of grinning dignitaries or thousands of identikit faces at Megacorp™ Arenas: instead we get the neighbourhood exuberance of St Paul's Carnival and the eccentricity of the West's best alternative music festivals, Ashton Court and Glastonbury. This interest in things at grassroots level is perhaps best seen in the series of pictures documenting the demonstrations against Margaret Thatcher's fatally unpopular Poll Tax in 1990-91. Mark followed the campaign from its beginnings in early 1990, onwards to the great London demonstrations.

Mark Simmons is interested in narrative, in people, in social change, in the political background to his pictures: in that way he is a photojournalist as well as a photographer, and often a social polemicist into the bargain. These pictures may not have you cooing at technicolour sunsets, enigmatic looks or dawn mist dancing across limpid water: yes, they are beautifully constructed images, but you always sense that the aesthetics of the picture are only as important as whatever Mark wishes to illustrate about the scene – about these people, this community, that political climate. It takes a fairly single-minded photographer, after all, to devote five years of his life to seeking out, acquiring the trust of and spending long hours with a variety of religious communities; or, indeed, to stand inches from the barricades and batons at the Poll Tax riots – even to go so far as sustaining a bang on the head for his tenacity.

Mark is setting scenes, telling stories and inviting debate with his photographs. For example, just look at the drama and narrative in the images in the 'Protest' chapter of demonstrators and police squaring up. Here again, composition comes to the aid of the message the picture presses home. The image is divided straight down the centre by the fence that flimsily separates the two groups: a striking portrayal of the implacable opposition of the two groups.

In the messages they convey and the facets of human behaviour, beliefs and social change that they illustrate, Mark's photographs are often as much visual parables as anything else. These pictures have codes that aren't accidental and aren't even particularly about the aesthetic rules of photography. Instead, the positions people take, their body language and stances illustrate timeless human themes: loyalty, conflict, community, celebration, sensuality, the oppressor and the oppressed. In that way, although these are pictures of a certain place at a certain time, we can call Mark's images truly timeless.

Steve Wright
Art Editor, Venue Magazine

"Think for yourselves and let others enjoy the privilege to do so too."
Voltaire, *Essay on Tolerance*

SUNDAY LEAGUE
Hopetoun Road, St
Werburgh's, January 1989

✱ It was a very misty morning and the road had just been re-surfaced so there were no road markings and virtually no cars giving this picture a romantic, timeless quality. An iconic shot of boys being boys.

DANNY'S TATTOO PARLOUR
Mina Road, St Werburgh's, February 1989

✱ Danny Skuse's renowned tattoo parlour. Now a men's hostel
- as with life, everything changes.

ME
Workers from Barton Hill Settlement Café, June 1989

✱ I photographed the boy first because he had a black eye. Then I asked the girl if I could take her photo: she said 'no' and immediately covered her face with the magazine which is when I got the shot. The image asks all sorts of questions about beauty, identity and who is the real 'me'.

BUS SHELTER
Cheltenham Road,
August, 1991

✱ We are bombarded by advertising messages which often rely on images of women. Women are constantly misrepresented in the media and the advertisers even hijack our public spaces.

17

ON THE EDGE OF LOVE
Easton, April 1989

✤ Quintessential lovely old ladies. The clincher is the book she's holding: *On the Edge of Love.* She's clasping the book like a teenager clutching a precious love letter.

BUTCHERS
Chandos Road, Redland, June 1987

✱ I just stop people and ask them if I can take their photograph. Then it's about
the chemistry between me and them and what that produces.

MAN AND DOG
Lawrence Hill, June 1989

✱ This is a portrait of unquestioning co-dependency. The animal peers suspiciously at the camera. I went down low to take this photograph so that I was at the dog's eye level. They often say people grow to resemble their pets – in this shot they both peer at me with the same quizzical look.

MEN SMOKING
Holy Trinity Church, Hotwells, Autumn 1985

MEN ON ALLOTMENTS
St Werburgh's, January 1989

CLAW
St Werburgh's Scrap Yard, February 1989

✸ This worker is going about his business unaware of the
looming presence of the mechanical claw just behind him.

CRASH
Sevier Street, St Werburgh's, December 1988

✱ I was discussing the accident with my mechanic friend
Nick when Henry came along to add his opinion.

BRISTOL DIOCESE
MOTHERS' UNION
The Haymarket, May 1991

✱ The Mothers' Union were packing an aid container headed for a community centre in Uganda – ordinary people just getting on with what needs to be done. You can see their various personalities and feel the pleasure of work, of getting stuck in to the task.

MAJORETTES
Bristol Harbourside, July 1989

SUNDAY WORSHIP
Eastville, May 1990

✱ Bristol Rovers fans celebrate promotion and winning the Division
Three championship. All are caught in collective celebration.

BOUNCY CASTLE
*Malcolm X Centre, St Paul's,
July 1991*

✱ I like photographing unaffected
people. Kids respond particularly to
directness and they are direct back.

31

BOYS' TOYS
Victoria Park, Bath, October 1990

✱ This was taken at a recruitment stand at a Police and Army Fair. The boy in the
foreground is completely absorbed in battle while the other boy looks on unnerved.
The men behind are tense and uneasy. Then there's the army instructor
oblivious to the whole thing.

BOY SMOKING
Southmead Youth Centre, October 1994

FRUIT MACHINES
Mad Harry's Amusement Arcade, Nelson Street, July 1989

PLEASE...
Whiteladies Road, December 1994

✱ A portrait of a life (anxiety, paranoia, persecution) in one brief note.

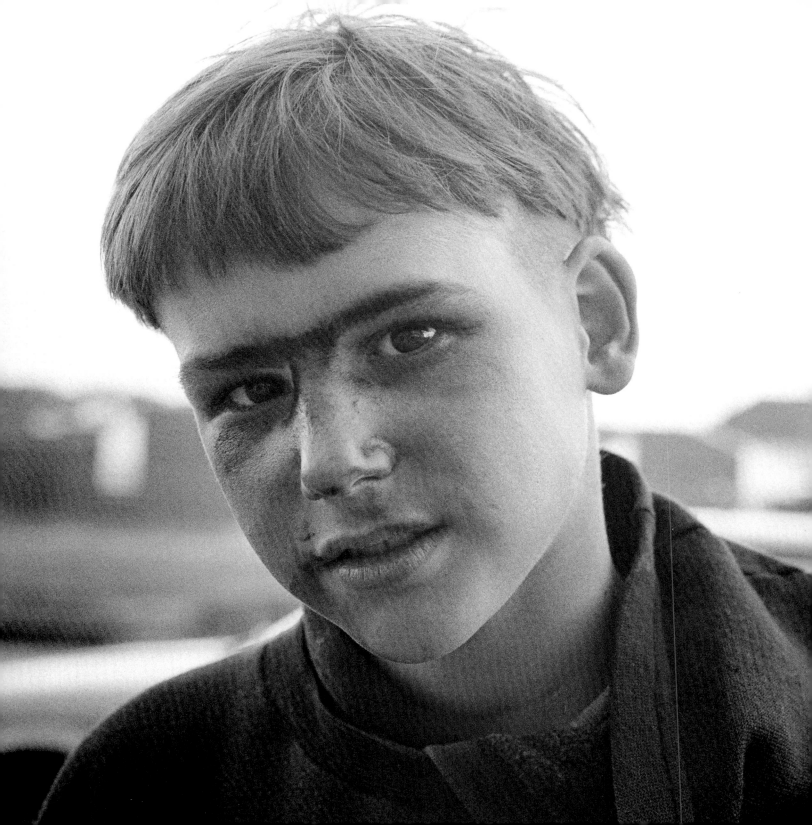

SOUTHMEAD BOYS
Greystoke Avenue, May 1994

✱ The boy in the foreground looks almost tribal with his basin haircut and smudged dirt markings on his face. There's a real depth and openness in his eyes. It's his friend in the background who brings a tension to the scene.

FAN CLUB
Victoria Rooms, May 1989

✳ A moment of anxious preparation and expectation backstage at the Floyd Fashion Show. The main model looks uncertain as the others will her on. The figure to the left looks aloof, detached from all the drama.

MEN BEHAVING BADLY
Revolution Bar, George Street, Bath, April 2004

✱ A classic beer-bellied bloke looks quizzically at the camera while behind
him the two girls are in hysterics. They're seeing what we're seeing.

RAW

Club Loco, Hepburn Road, May 1995

✱ A club night called RAW seems quite appropriate. There's a charged atmosphere
of sexualised, physical energy, but also a sense of
fun and innocence in this photo.

43

BODY HEAT
Conscious Club, Trinity
Centre, July 1994

✳ An assignment for the clubbing
pages of *Venue* magazine. The night
was so hot that I had to wait an
hour for my camera to acclimatise
to the heat before I could start
taking photos.

JUNGLE FEVER
Gass Club, London, February 1995

✱ Shooting of a Jungle music promotional video.

BOGLE COMPETITION
Easton Community Centre, October 1992

✱ A Jamaican Bogle dance competition at the local community centre.
The young man looks completely rapt, his partner is serene and
holding the space while the crowd cheers them on.

47

SPEAKERS CORNER
Grosvenor Road speaker stack, St Paul's Carnival, July 1991

SOUND SYSTEM
Outside the former Crystal Dove Night Club,
St Paul's Carnival, July 1998

✱ Carnival comes around once a year and for Bristolians it's a special time: the streets are
theirs for the day. At the time this picture was taken, Banksy was spraying a mural on the
back of the building. Both building and mural are now gone.

49

RONI SIZE
Tribal Gathering,
Otmoor Park, Oxfordshire,
May 1995

PERFORMERS
St Paul's Carnival, July 2005

CROWD
St Paul's Carnival, July 2000

FOOD
St Paul's Carnival, July 1991

55

SOUND SYSTEM
Black & White Café, St Paul's Carnival, July 1998

✱ The first picture I took of this guy, he was looking quite mean. Then he seemed to warm to me: he smiled and winked and I had my shot.

SAMBA PROCESSION
City Road, St Paul's Carnival, July 1998

✱ Bristol School of Samba.

SKETCH SHOW
Glastonbury Festival, June 1989

✱ Late night cabaret show. Just the sort of madness
you encounter on Glastonbury's outer reaches.

HORSEMEN OF THE APOCALYPSE
WOMAD Festival, July 2000

✱ Maybe it's not that serious after all…

'IRON JOHN' MEN'S CAMP
Wales, June 1992

✱ A visit to a men's camp inspired by Robert Bly's *Iron John: A Book About Men*,
which focuses on men's emotional and psychological wellbeing. I found a very
uncomplicated, innocent atmosphere full of simple companionship.

FREE FESTIVAL
Ashton Court Festival Bristol, July 2000

✱ A scene from the legendary Ashton Court Festival. An image that
sums up the anything-goes energy at Europe's biggest free festival.

MUD WRESTLING
Teepee Field, Glastonbury Festival, June 2007

✱ Veterans of muddy Glastonbury know how to have fun.

DOWNTIME
Glastonbury Festival, June 1998

✱ After the highs… the lows. Shortly after this picture was taken, the man was
rescued by the brilliant First Aiders who pick up the pieces at the festival.

BARKING
FUCKING MAD
Glastonbury Festival,
June 1998

✱ Another year of mud: a regular
and notorious Glastonbury feature.
In the background, a sign reads
'Dreamtime' suggesting both the
dream and the reality of this
great festival.

BAILIFF WATCH
Barry, South Wales, August 1990

✱ Residents keep vigil against the expected arrival of bailiffs demanding
Poll Tax payments. A portrait of defiance across the generations.

DEVIL'S WORK
Anti-Poll Tax demonstration, Brockwell Park, London, October 1990

✱ 'Poll Tax Will Add To Crime' reads the banner prophetically.
Nearby, the Devil is eating a sandwich.

PEACEFUL PROTEST
*Anti–Poll Tax
demonstration, Greyfriars,
Bristol, April 1990*

✱ The Poll Tax united people from
across political, age and class
divides. This regressive tax – Britain
had not had a poll tax since 1381 –
was one step too far even for
Margaret Thatcher, who had
epitomised the 'greed is good'
1980s and championed self-interest
over social cohesion. The unrest
created by the tax was instrumental
in Thatcher's downfall in November
of that year.

BRITISH FARCE AT ITS BEST

Anti-Poll Tax demonstration, Whitehall, London, March 1990

✱ Police pushing protesters up towards Trafalgar Square. Why? The theatrical
backdrop comments on the comedy and slapstick nature of the scene.

NO POLL TAX!

Anti-Poll Tax demonstration, Whitehall, London, March 1990

✱ The largest of the anti-Poll Tax demonstrations, with 200,000 protesters converging on London. This was just before the start of the trouble as people marched up Whitehall.

**SOME CAME PREPARED
FOR TROUBLE**
*Anti-Poll Tax
demonstration,
Whitehall, London,
March 1990*

✱ A headline the following day
read, 'Some Came Prepared for
Trouble'. I was never quite sure who
they were referring to.

ARREST
Anti-Poll Tax demonstration, College Green, March 1990

INJURED POLICEMAN
Anti-Poll Tax demonstration, Whitehall, London, March 1990

✱ The Police look apprehensive as they run past an injured colleague. I was hit on the
head with a truncheon just for taking photographs at this protest.

77

STUFF MAGGIE
Anti-Poll Tax demonstration, College Green, March 1990

BURNING ISSUE
Burning of Poll Tax demands, College Green, April 1990

✱ The sheer numbers of people defying the Tax, demonstrating and clogging up the
courts finally made the Poll Tax unworkable and spelt the end for Maggie Thatcher.
People power in action.

GATHERING STORM
*Anti-Poll Tax
demonstration,
Whitehall, London,
March 1990*

✱ Just after the start of the conflicts,
police and protesters face off over
a flimsy dividing barrier. This is
the last stage of dialogue before
the riots kick off in earnest.
The police send in the horses;
the troubles escalate.

FORBIDDEN PLANET
March for National Aids Awareness Day, central Bristol,
December 1990

OPERATION DELIVERY
Grosvenor Road, St Paul's, Bristol, September 1986

★ Police carry out a drugs raid of the infamous Black and White Café.
Councillors accused Assistant Chief Constable Malcolm Popperwell
of staging a 'semi-military' operation.

UNDER SIEGE
Nation of Islam presence at the Notting Hill Carnival, London,
August 1997

WAR IS TERROR

Anti-war demonstration, London, February 2003

✱ Huge numbers (estimates vary from 750,000 to 2 million) protest against the invasion of Iraq. The banner shows how our leaders play with words in an Orwellian fashion.

ZOMBIES
Cabot Circus, Bristol, September 2008

✱ There was bound to be a protest at the hundreds of millions of pounds spent on
building the new Cabot Circus shopping centre in Bristol. This demonstration
spoke for many Bristolians.

ZOMBIES
Cabot Circus, Bristol, September 2008

✱ Apart from confusing the police and security guards, the Zombie March was also a
reference to George A. Romero's anti-consumerism horror movie *The Day of the Dead*.

PRAYER

Church of God of Prophecy,
Tudor Rd, Easton,
September 1992

✱ Pastor Feron and his congregation were always very welcoming and accommodating on my many visits to his church. I particularly enjoyed the music and the sense of community.

PASSION OF CHRIST
Broadmead shopping centre, January 1989

RASTAFARIAN GIRLS STUDYING BIBLE
Easton, October 1992

✱ It was quite difficult finding Rastafarian contacts who were willing to be photographed.
In meeting Ras B, Morowa and family I was very fortunate and we have remained
friends ever since.

INTERFAITH
CANDLELIT VIGIL
College Green,
September 1990

✱ I like the different expressions in
this photograph. The kids in the
foreground are exuberant, excited;
behind them, the adults seem more
guarded and circumspect. It shows
religion as a way of expressing
wonder and awe at life.

94

TABLE TURNING
Bristol's First Spiritualist Church, Surrey Street, September 1992

✷ This image shows the table leaning over substantially. It was actually moving pretty
wildly and I could not see any way that it was being manipulated.

SUNDAY SERVICE
Church of God of Prophecy, Tudor Road, Easton, December 1990

**MOSQUE BY
MOONLIGHT**
*Bristol Jamia Mosque,
Totterdown, February 1992*

MOSQUE PRAYERS
Bristol Jamia Mosque, Totterdown, July 1991

✱ It was fairly difficult gaining trust and access to the Mosque because my initial contacts
coincided with the 'first' Gulf war and worshippers were understandably
cautious of my intentions.

EID GREETINGS
Bristol Jamia Mosque, Totterdown, April 1992

DIWALI
Hindu Temple, Church Road, Redfield, October 1990

✷ A quiet moment from the winter 'Festival of Light' service. The celebrations at the Hindu
temple were the most exuberant that I attended during the Faith project.

MISTY MORNING
Birdcage Walk cemetery, Clifton, December 1990

JACOB
Corfu, September 1994

✸ My son Jacob illuminated by
flames. We made his hair into little
horns to add to the devilish look.

106

MASSIVE ATTACK
Fire Station studio, October 2001

✱ Photo-shoot for magazine exclusive.

DJ QUEEN BEE
Publicity photo, by Clifton Suspension Bridge, March 1997

✱ Bristol's foremost female DJ

SUB LOVE
Easton, March 1992

✱ Early 1990s Bristol hip-hop crew featuring Jody Wisternoff and DJ Die from Roni Size's Full Cycle label. Photographed for a Venue magazine feature. Pictured left to right: Alex Swift, Jody, Markus Lewis (back), Faye Jones and Die.

RONI SIZE AND KRUST
Brigstocke Road, January 1996

✱ Bristol drum and bass duo photographed for *Straight No Chaser* magazine.
As Reprazent, they would go on to win the Mercury Prize in 1997
for their album *New Forms*.

CARLTON MCCARTHY
Watershed, Autumn 1987

✱ Bristol singer who, the following year, would sing on the first
Massive Attack/Smith & Mighty release, *Any Love*.

ROB SMITH
Promotional photograph, Fire Station Studio, October 2003

✱ Prolific producer and DJ, one half of the seminal duo Smith & Mighty
and in no small part responsible for the 'Bristol Sound'.

SI JOHN
Promotional photograph, Fire Station studio, April 2001

✴ Bass supremo and producer, responsible for the unforgettable
bass line on Reprazent's *Brown Paper Bag*.

JOHN STAPLETON, AKA DR JAM
Ashton Court Festival, July 1987

✱ Founding father of Def Con and Bristol's legendary club night Blowpop, seen here in his early days DJing with another local musical institution – The Blue Aeroplanes.

3D
Monks Park School, Horfield, November 2001

✱ Massive Attack's 3D, photographed for Another Magazine outside his old school.

SOUND BWOY
St Paul's Carnival, July 1991

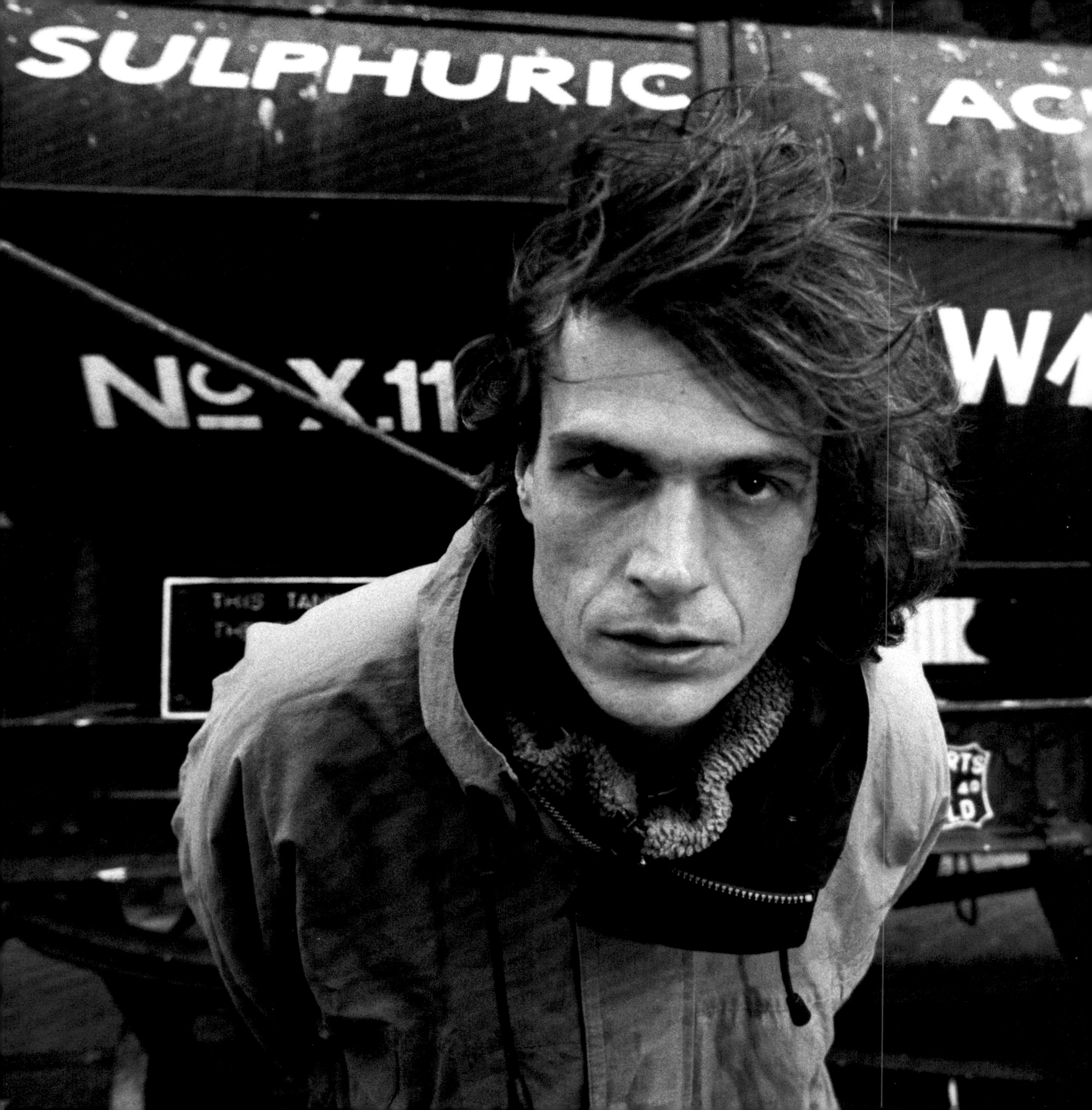
SULPHURIC

LUPINE HOWL
Press photograph, Bristol Industrial Museum, May 2000

✱ Lupine Howl was formed from three members of Spiritualized: Mike Mooney and Sean Cook (pictured) plus Damon Reece. The three were ousted from Spititalized shortly after their mega-selling album *Ladies and Gentlemen We Are Floating in Space.*

SPAWN STARS
Publicity photograph for Natural Theatre Company, October 2002

✱ Bath's veteran street-theatre troupe, the Natural Theatre Company,
are seen rehearsing their latest madcap comedy *In The Eyes of Cod*.

CARD SHARP
Lindsay Hart of Bristol circus troupe Circus Malabaristas,
Fire Station studio, February 2003

MINNIE WITH WEDDING PHOTO
Outside Watershed, Autumn 1987

TICKET TO NOWHERE
Stoke Gifford community play, by acta, April 1998